Flute Time Christmas

a stockingful of 32 easy pieces for flute

Kathy and David Blackwell

with Caroline Hobbs-Smith

illustrations by Alan Rowe

T0057004

Welcome to **Flute Time Christmas**. You'll find:

- 32 well-known Christmas carols and pieces with words to sing along
- solos and duets
- easy chord symbols for guitar or keyboard accompaniment; these chords are not compatible with the CD performances
- a CD with performances to listen or play along to; the varied accompaniments use piano, guitar, drums, and bass
- piano accompaniments available in a separate volume

Using the CD:

- all carols and pieces are played through twice, except those pieces which include a **D.C.** or **D.S. al Fine**, 'Skaters' Waltz', and 'Hogmanay Reel', which are performed once only
- each carol and piece has a short introduction and a link between the verses
- where there are duet parts, these are mostly added in the second verse
- Tuning track: track 33.

Performers: flute Caroline Hobbs-Smith; guitar Jez Cook; double bass/bass guitar Mike Chilcott; percussion/drum kit Ben Twyford; piano David Blackwell.

MUSIC DEPARTMENT

OXFORD
UNIVERSITY PRESS

OXFORD
UNIVERSITY PRESS

Great Clarendon Street, Oxford OX2 6DP, England

Oxford University Press is a department of the University of Oxford.
It furthers the University's aim of excellence in research, scholarship,
and education by publishing worldwide

Oxford is a registered trade mark of Oxford University Press
in the UK and in certain other countries

This collection © Oxford University Press 2001 and 2011

Kathy and David Blackwell have asserted their rights under
the Copyright, Designs and Patents Act, 1988, to be identified as
Composers of this Work

Database right Oxford University Press (maker)

First published 2011
Photocopying or arranging this copyright material is ILLEGAL

All rights reserved. No part of this publication may be reproduced,
stored in a retrieval system, or transmitted, in any form or by any means,
without the prior permission in writing of Oxford University Press,
or as expressly permitted by law. Enquiries concerning reproduction
outside the scope of the above should be sent to the Music Copyright
Department, Oxford University Press, at the address above

Permission to perform these works in public
(except in the course of divine worship) should normally be obtained
from the Performing Right Society Ltd (PRS), 29/33 Berners Street,
London W1T 3AB, or its affiliated Societies in each country throughout
the world, unless the owner or the occupier of the premises
being used holds a licence from the Society

Permission to make a recording must be obtained in advance
from the Mechanical-Copyright Protection Society Ltd (MCPS),
Elgar House, 41 Streatham High Road, London SW16 1ER,
or its affiliated Societies in each country throughout the world

9 10 8

ISBN 978-0-19-337927-5

Music and text origination by
Katie Johnston
Printed in Great Britain on acid-free paper by
Halstan & Co. Ltd, Amersham, Bucks.

Contents

Piece/ track no.		Page no.
1	*Hark! the herald-angels sing	4
2	Mary had a baby	4
3	The holly and the ivy (*duet*)	5
4	Ding dong! merrily on high	6
5	*Andrew mine, Jasper mine	6
6	Silent night (*duet*)	7
7	I saw three ships (*duet*)	8
8	*O little town of Bethlehem	8
9	Christmas Calypso (*duet*)	9
10	*Once in royal David's city	10
11	Go tell it on the mountain	10
12	O Christmas tree (*duet*)	11
13	We wish you a merry Christmas	12
14	Shepherds watched	12
15	We three kings	13
16	*O come, all ye faithful (*duet*)	14
17	Bethl'em lay a-sleeping (*duet*)	15
18	Deck the hall	16
19	Good King Wenceslas	16
20	Away in a manger (*duet*)	17
21	*The first Nowell	17
22	Zither Carol	18
23	God rest you merry, gentlemen	18
24	*While shepherds watched their flocks	19
25	Children, go! (*duet*)	19
26	Dance of the Reed Pipes	20
27	Skaters' Waltz (*duet*)	21
28	*Jingle, bells	22
29	Infant holy, infant lowly (*duet*)	22
30	Child in a manger (*duet*)	23
31	Hogmanay Reel	24
32	Auld Lang Syne	24
33	Tuning track (A)	

* These carols can be played an octave higher for the second verse.

1. Hark! the herald-angels sing

Felix Mendelssohn (1809–47)

Joyfully

G *mf* D G C G D G *mp*

Hark! the he - rald - an-gels sing_ Glo - ry to the new-born King; Peace on earth and

A7 D A7 D A7 D *f* G C G D

mer - cy mild,_ God and sin - ners re - con-ciled: Joy - ful all ye na-tions rise,_

G C G D C Am E7 Am D7 G

Join the tri-umph of the skies, With the'an-gel - ic host pro-claim, Christ is_ born in

G D G *ff* C Am E7 Am D7 G G D G

Beth - le - hem. Hark! the he - rald - an - gels sing Glo - ry__ to the new-born King.

2. Mary had a baby

American trad.

Lively

B♭ *mf* E♭ F B♭ E♭ F

Ma-ry had a ba - by, Yes, Lord! Ma-ry had a ba - by, Yes, my Lord!

B♭ E♭ B♭ *f* F B♭

Ma-ry had a ba - by, Yes, Lord! Peo-ple keep a-com-in', and the train done gone!

3. The holly and the ivy

English trad.

4. Ding dong! merrily on high

16th-century French melody

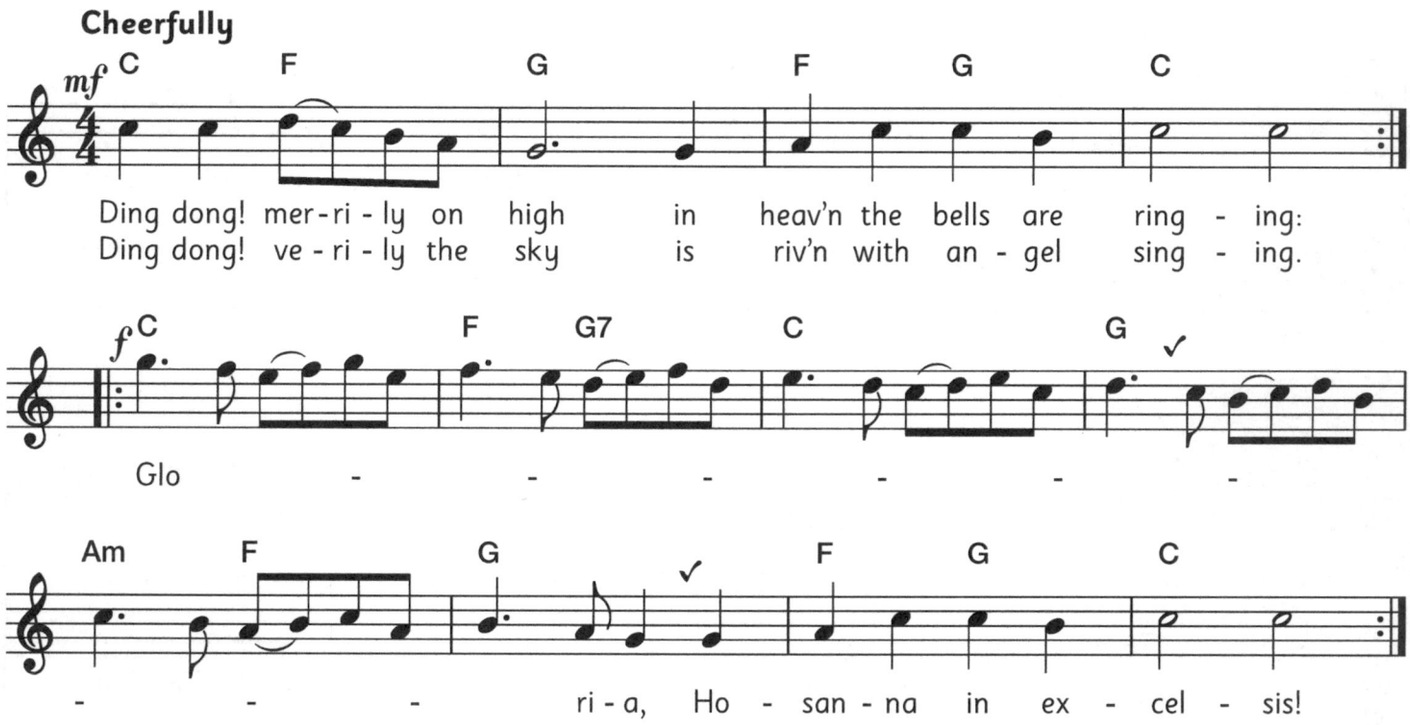

5. Andrew mine, Jasper mine

Moravian carol

Andrew mine, Jasper mine: words by C. K. Offer from *Three Moravian Carols* © Oxford University Press 1962. Reproduced by permission of Oxford University Press.

6. Silent night

Franz Gruber (1787–1863)

Tenderly

D A7

mp

Si - lent night, ho - ly night, All is calm,

mp

D G D

all is bright; Round yon vir - gin mo - ther and child.

G D A7

mf

Ho - ly in - fant so ten - der and mild, Sleep in

mf

D A7 D

mp

hea - ven-ly peace, Sleep in hea - ven-ly peace.

mp

7. I saw three ships

English trad.

8. O little town of Bethlehem

English trad.

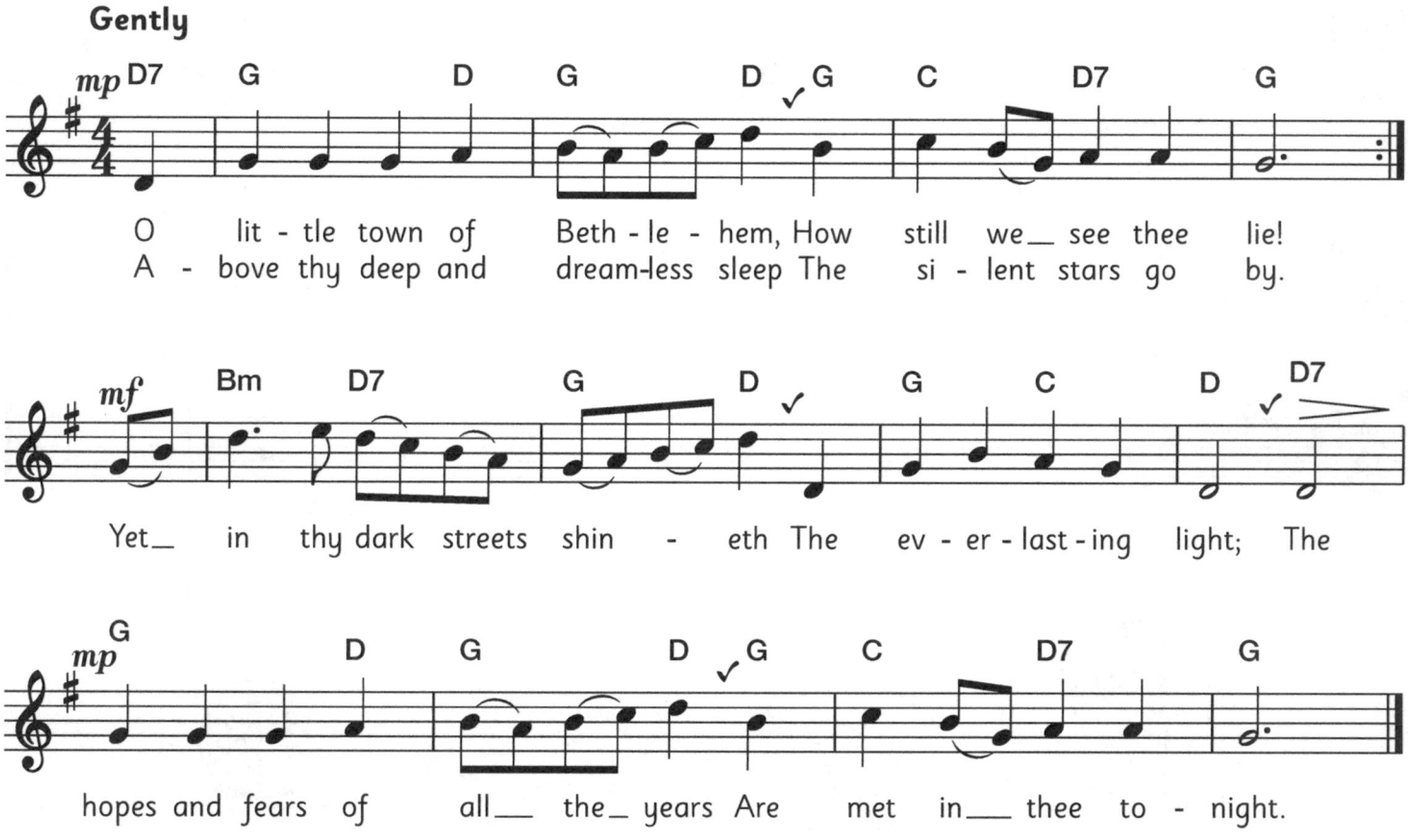

9. Christmas Calypso

Kathy & David Blackwell

10. Once in royal David's city

H. J. Gauntlett (1805–76)

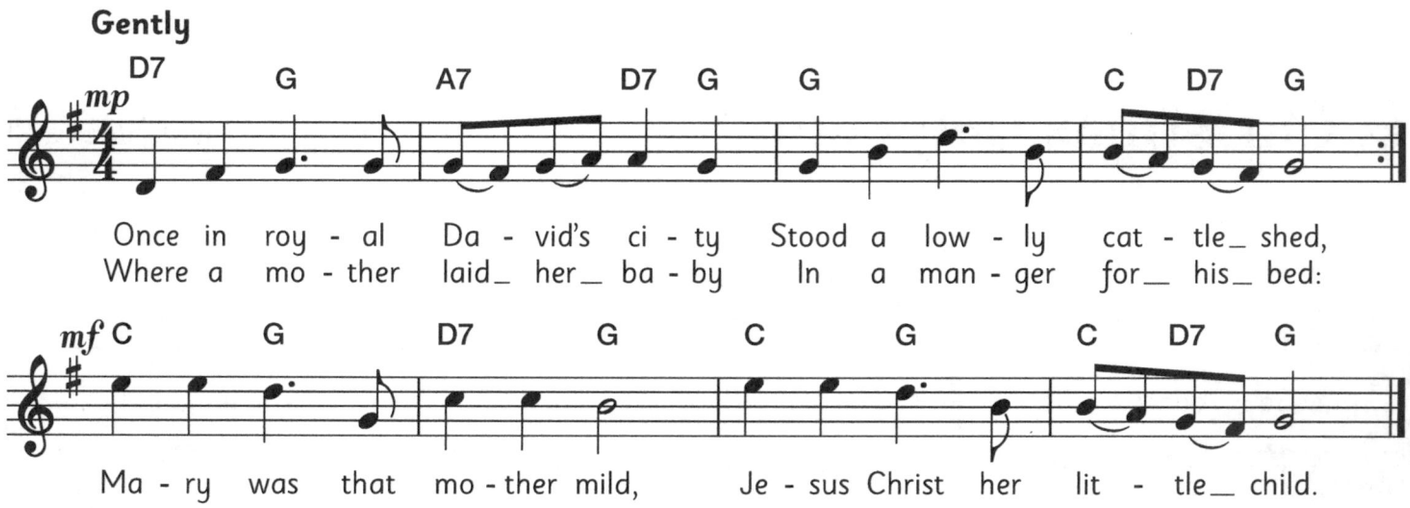

11. Go tell it on the mountain

American trad.

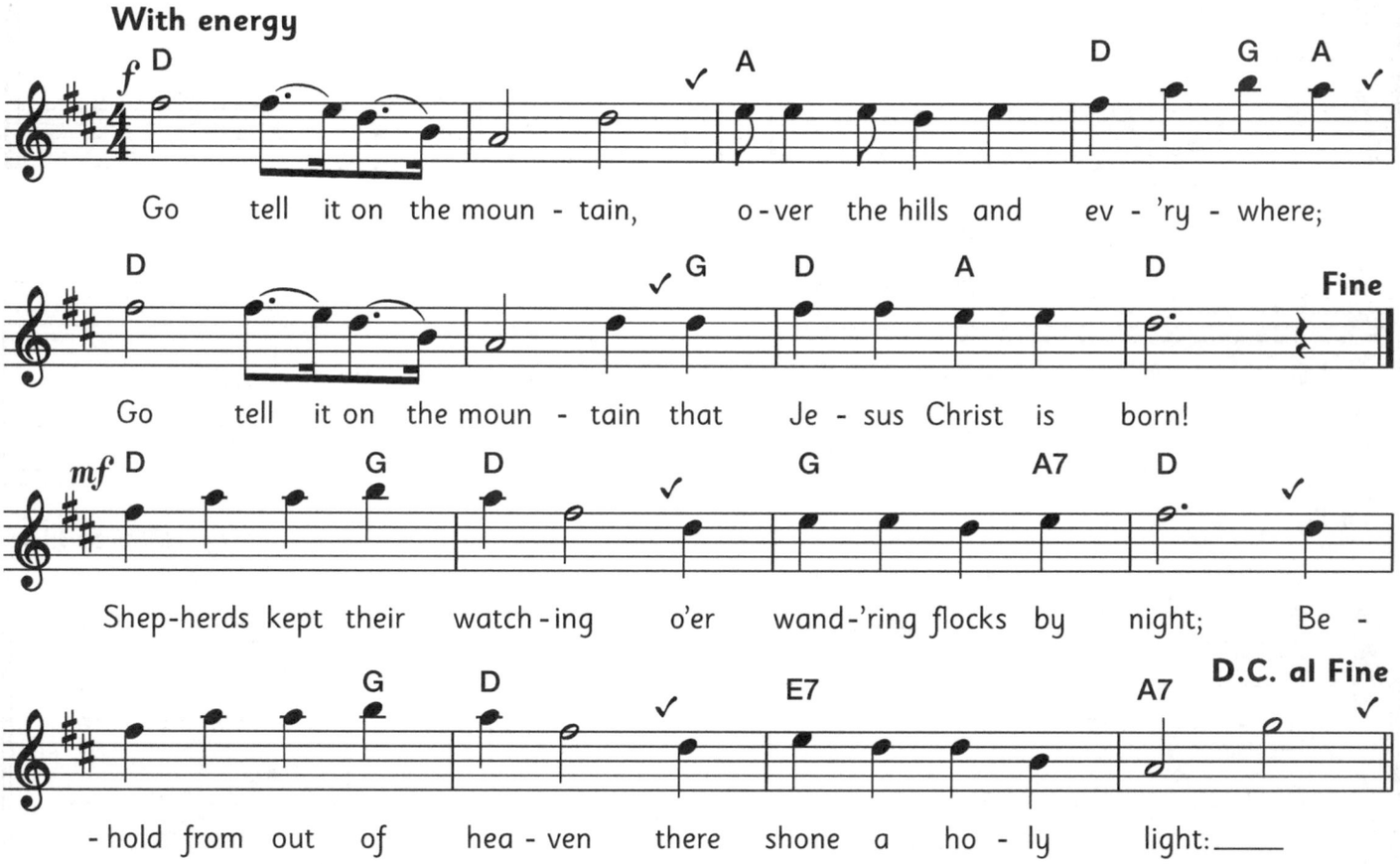

12. O Christmas tree

German trad.

13. We wish you a merry Christmas

trad. West Country

14. Shepherds watched

Czech carol

15. We three kings

J. H. Hopkins (1820–91)

On the move

16. O come, all ye faithful

J. F. Wade (*c.*1711–86)

17. Bethl'em lay a-sleeping

Polish carol

Simply

mp

Beth - l'em lay a - sleep - ing, long, so long a - go,

mp

Twink - ling stars were peep - ing, long, so long a - go,

When to earth a ba - by came, lit - tle Je - sus was his name, long, long a - go.

18. Deck the hall

Welsh trad.

19. Good King Wenceslas

Piae Cantiones (1582)

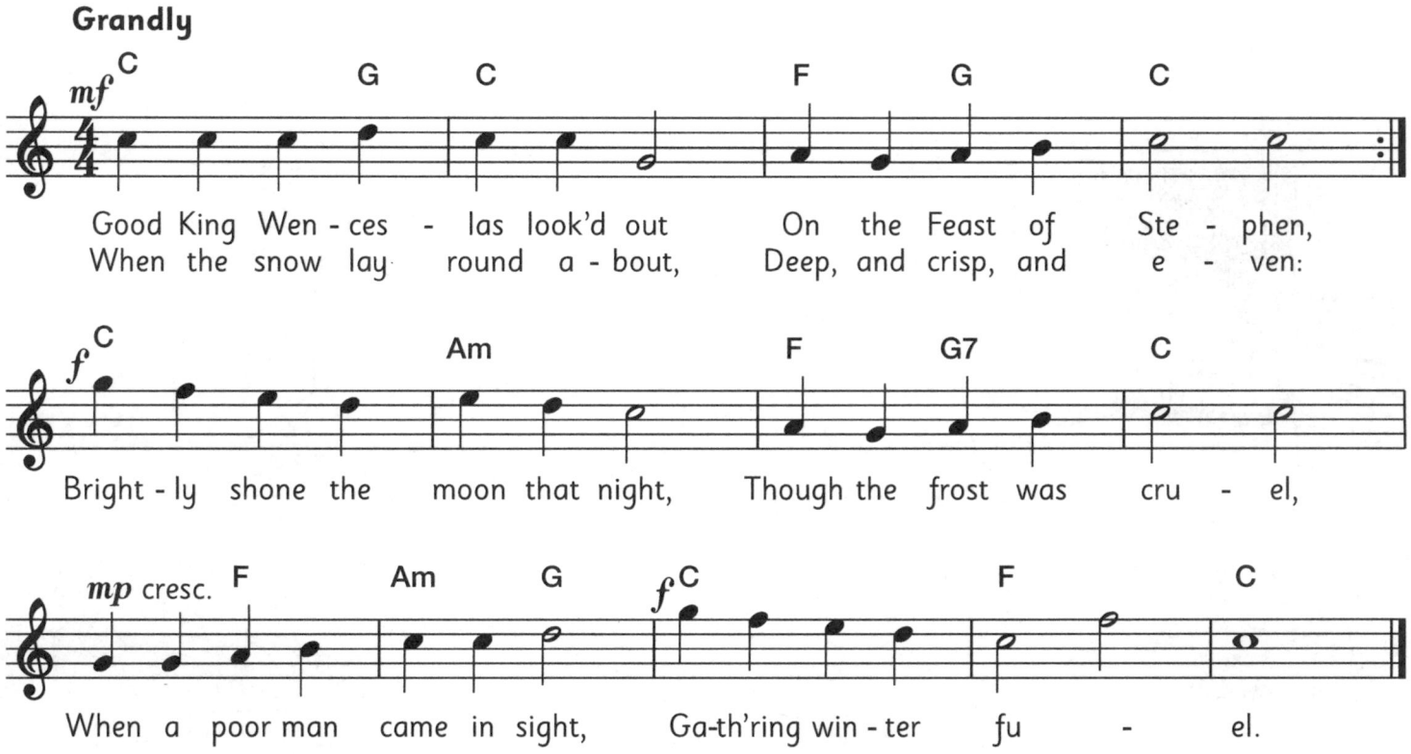

20. Away in a manger

William J. Kirkpatrick (1838–1921)

21. The first Nowell

English trad.

22. Zither Carol

Czech carol

23. God rest you merry, gentlemen

English trad.

24. While shepherds watched their flocks

Este's Psalter (1592)

25. Children, go!

Spiritual

26. Dance of the Reed Pipes

(from the *Nutcracker* ballet)

Pyotr Ilyich Tchaikovsky (1840–93)

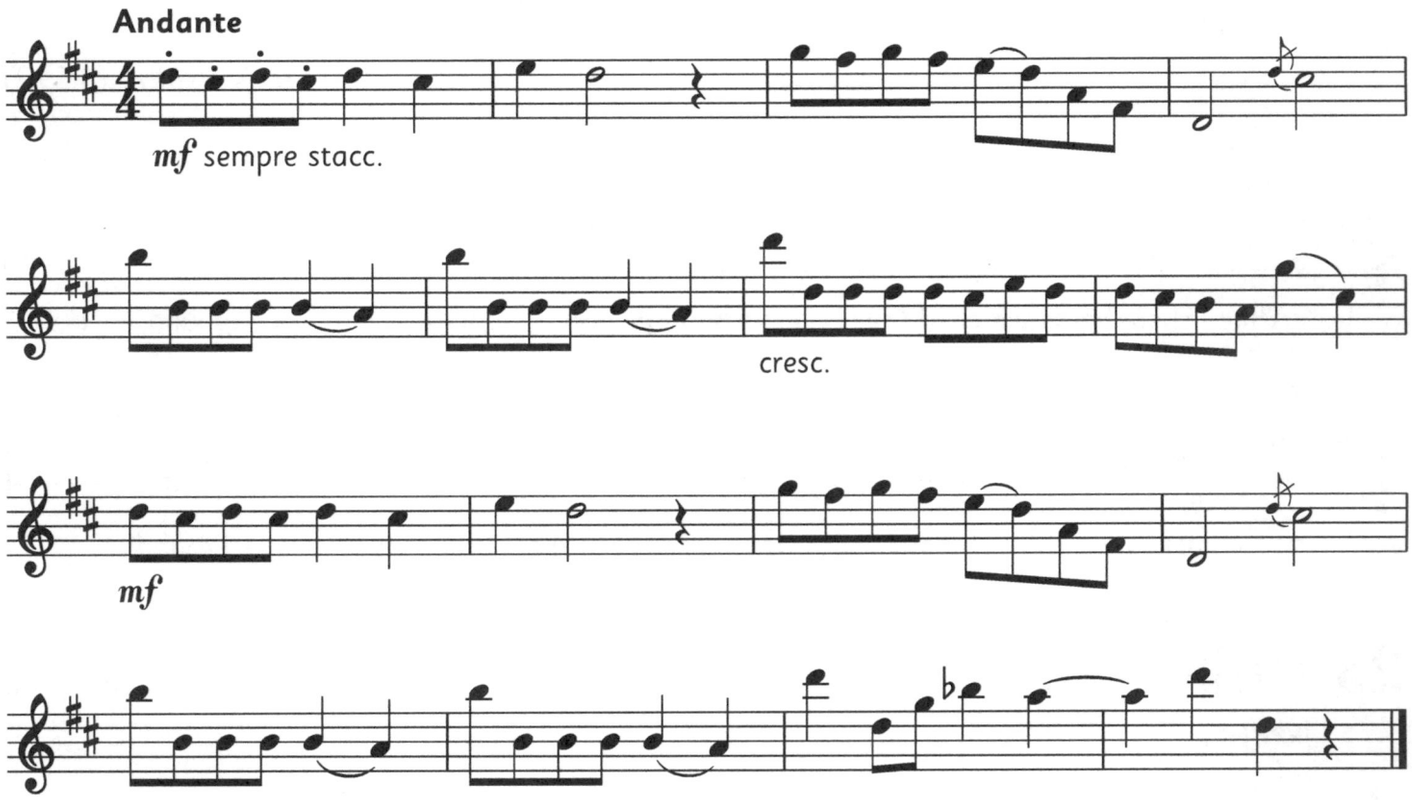

27. Skaters' Waltz

Emil Waldteufel (1837–1915)

28. Jingle, bells

J. Pierpont (1822–93)

29. Infant holy, infant lowly

Polish carol

30. Child in a manger

Celtic trad.

31. Hogmanay Reel

Kathy & David Blackwell

With energy

32. Auld Lang Syne

Scottish trad.

With a wee dram!

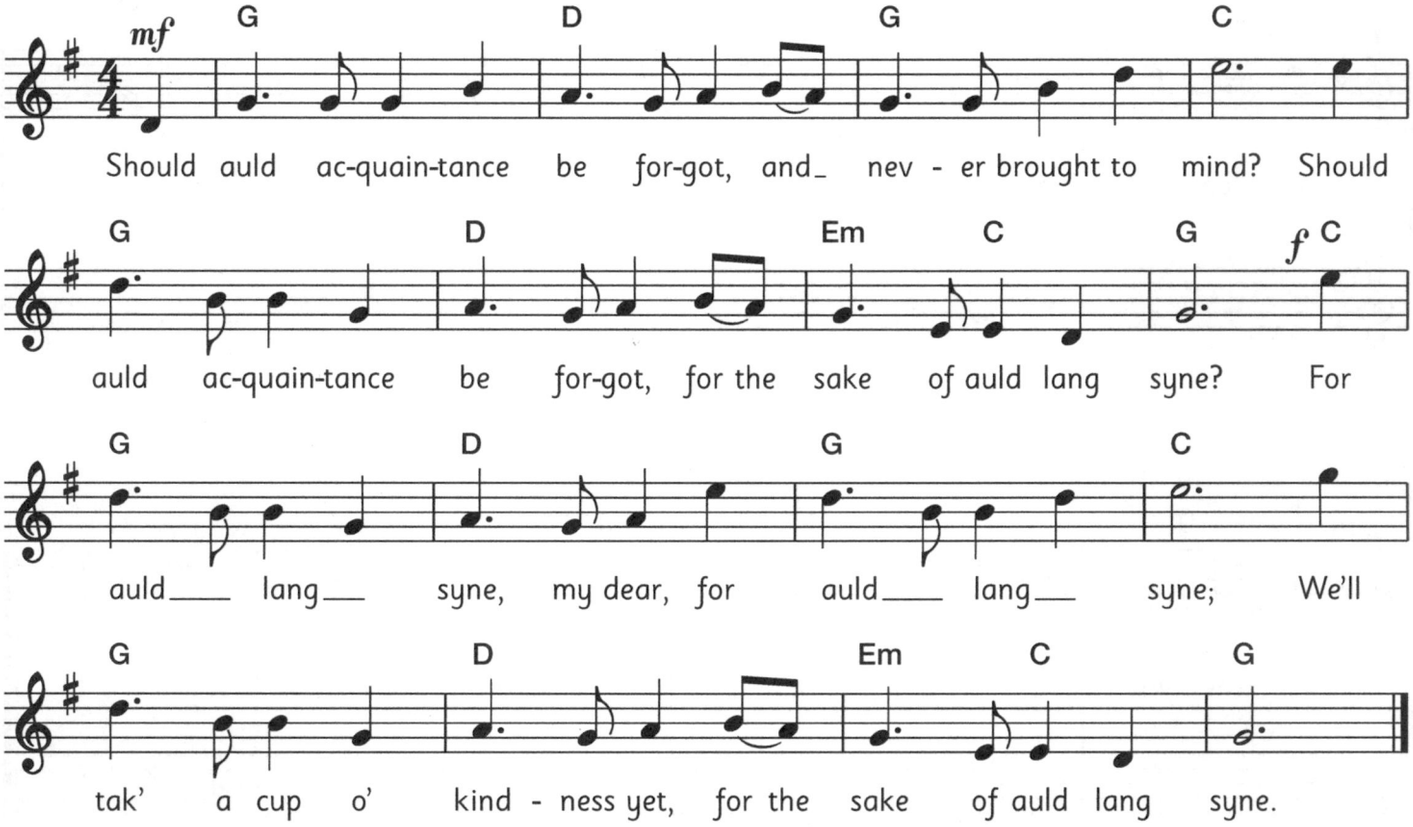